Other Books by

Adèle Lang and Susi Rajah

How to Spot a Bastard by His Star Sign

By Adèle Lang

Confessions of a Sociopathic Social Climber

I'm not a feminist, but . . .

03 04 05 06 07 WKT 10 9 8 7 6 5 4 3 2 1

ISBN: 0-7407-3903-4

Library of Congress Catalog Card Number: 2003102701

Design by Susi Rajah

I'm not a feminist, but . . .

Adèle Lang and Susi Rajah

**Andrews McMeel
Publishing**

Kansas City

Is it because women burned their bras that they now have to put silicon in their breasts?

Why are men allowed to go topless in public even when some of them have bigger breasts than women?

Why isn't there a
tacky restaurant chain
called Peckers?

If men are better drivers than women, why do they have more accidents?

Why is doing anything
"like a girl" a bad thing—
even for a girl?

Why aren't there any

father-in-law jokes?

Why aren't blond men considered intellectually challenged?

Why is there a children's game called Old Maid in which the loser gets stuck with the Old Maid?

How come no one can remember a popular female Muppet who lived on Sesame Street?

How come the most lucrative endorsement deals go to the best-performing male athletes and the best-looking female ones?

If men are so into sports,

why is the biggest selling

issue of *Sports Illustrated*

the swimsuit edition?

If men buy *Playboy* for the articles, why does the magazine go to the trouble of printing pictures of naked women?

Why is there never any real difference between the picture on the cover of *Cosmo* and the picture on the cover of *Maxim*?

Why do men's magazines print articles on how to get ahead while women's magazines print articles on how to perform fellatio?

Why don't men write to magazines for advice on juggling family and career?

Do guys who find women who drink unattractive think men get better looking with every beer?

If men don't like drunk women, why do they try to get women drunk?

Why, when men say they don't understand women, are so many self-help books written by men and targeted at women?

Why isn't there a self-help book called *Men Who Screw Around Too Much?*

Why is it a man's world
when there are more
women than men in it?

Why are women accused of
man-bashing when it's women
who are battered by men?

Why do we use the word play*boy* to describe lecherous old men?

Why aren't young men warned to watch out for dirty old women?

Why is *master* a title of respect but *mistress* not?

Why is a bachelor

always eligible but a

spinster never so?

Why is the C-word the most
offensive insult known to man?

Why is calling someone a "mother" an affront?

Why is "sensitivity" attractive in a man when "aggression" is undesirable in a woman?

Is it because men have nothing to complain about that only women are "nags"?

Why are the reproductive
rights of young women
decided by old men?

Shouldn't the person who decides whether or not a woman has a baby be the one who has to push that eight-pound baby out of her vagina?

If women are so "manipulative," how come more of them aren't in politics?

Is it because men are led by their dicks that there are so many dicks in government?

Why is it that when you hold 51 percent of a company's stock you control the company, but if you make up 51 percent of society you don't control a thing?

Why is the most well-known woman to have run for president still Presidential Candidate Barbie?

If a woman ever got to be president of the United States, would her husband be called the first gentleman?

Is the president's wife called the first lady because she's the first in a long line of women he's involved with?

Why hasn't a woman held presidential office and a criminal has?

Why can't a woman be
a Catholic priest when a
pedophile can?

If men thought God was a woman, would they still kill and die for Her?

How many Islamic extremist men would blow themselves up if they were told feminists, not virgins, awaited them in heaven?

Why are all household cleaning products marketed to women?

Why is cooking "women's work" when the world's most celebrated chefs are men?

Why is it that only rich women can afford live-in child care when the poorest man can get it by marriage?

Why do men own 99 percent
of the world's property and
still expect women to do the
housework?

If men are more capable than women, why can't they perform simple household chores?

Why is it that the most effective labor-saving device for a man is a wife, but for a woman it's money?

Why aren't low-calorie

foods marketed to fat men?

Why is there anti-cellulite cream

but not anti-beer-belly cream?

Why do so many women think
throwing up their food makes
them look more attractive?

If women on the verge of starvation are the ideal of beauty, why aren't models recruited from famine-stricken countries?

Why do men claim they enjoy being with women with healthy appetites but admire the women who eat practically nothing?

Why aren't very thin men

considered sexy?

Why do only women have "vital statistics"?

Why can't actresses who are paid millions per movie afford to eat?

Why do size-four clothes have
to be pinned to fit mannequins?

Why is fashion always
designed for women
five inches taller and
forty pounds lighter?

Why do women have to wear makeup to achieve the "natural" look?

Why is razor stubble

sexy only on a man?

If men don't like women who are plastic and shallow, why is there a market for inflatable dolls?

If *The Stepford Wives* is fiction, why are life-size, anatomically correct dolls made to look like the woman of a man's choice available on the Internet?

How come only male TV anchors and hosts are allowed to be old and ugly?

Why do even the female victims of rape or murder have to be attractive to get media attention?

Why do female pop stars need to change their images while male pop stars need only change their songs?

Why do the most successful young female pop stars bear a striking resemblance to strippers?

Why are men allowed to openly voice their preference for large breasts yet expect women to pretend penis size doesn't matter?

Do men want women to have Barbie-like proportions because they want women so top-heavy they'd have to walk on all fours?

Why do women with low self-esteem cut themselves when a cosmetic surgeon could do it for them?

Why does a woman have to resort to plastic surgery to keep her youth while a man keeps his by giving her money, cars, and diamonds?

If ageism is a common problem for women and men, why don't more gray-haired men dye their hair?

If men lived longer than women, would senior citizens get a better deal from the government?

Why do sixty-year-old male actors get to play action heroes while female actors of the same age play their mothers?

Why does a twenty-two-year-old model have to pretend she is younger to get work?

Why, even though they have to cope with menopause, don't women have midlife crises?

Why do we say older women look
great for their age only when they
don't look their age?

Why are pedophiles sick,

but beauty pageants for

prepubescent girls not?

Do adult women wax off their pubic hair to attract the growing number of male pedophiles in the world?

How come there's such a push
for fathers' rights when
so many of them never stick
around to claim them?

Why don't single *dads*

have a bad name?

Why, in child-custody cases, are men with jobs regarded as good fathers whereas women with jobs are regarded as neglectful mothers?

If child rearing is the most

important job in the world,

why is it an unpaid position?

Why are the only two fields
in which women can outearn
men modeling and prostitution?

Why, when so many of them are accused of sleeping their way there, are there so few women at the top?

Why is the glass ceiling still intact and why don't they use the same kind of glass for windshields?

Why are the women who fly business class usually flight attendants?

Why is it men who mostly "work late" at the office when it's women who put in two-thirds of the world's work hours?

Why can a smart woman get
ahead by playing dumb?

If intelligent women are unaffected
by images in the media, why do a
quarter of female college students
develop eating disorders?

Are men given more promotions and pay raises at work to make them feel better about the fact they don't do as well as women at school, and are outnumbered by women at college?

Why has the strictly non-PC office calendar featuring topless women been replaced by hardcore porn on the Internet?

If pornography keeps sex offenders from offending, and seven hundred million porn tapes are rented each year, why are there still so many sex offenders?

If the porn industry really does promise freedom and power for women, why don't all little girls dream of becoming porn stars?

If porn is liberating for women, why do so many chauvinists approve of it?

Now that it's okay to show someone being shot in the head on TV, why is blue liquid still used to represent blood in sanitary napkin ads?

Why, in many places, are tampons and sanitary napkins priced like luxury goods?

Why did Viagra hit the market
before a male oral contraceptive?

Why is there an array of
contraceptive devices
for women and only
one for men?

Considering it's always been in the same place, why did it take so long to find the G-spot?

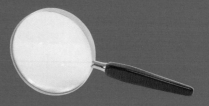

Is the reason women are still faking orgasms because men are still skipping foreplay?

Is it because men talk about themselves so much that women have headaches before sex?

Why is it that, even if they can't satisfy one woman in bed, men imagine they can satisfy two?

Why is it Hollywood thinks James Bond would happily have sex with a woman he knows is trying to kill him, but a woman needs to be offered a million dollars to get her to sleep with Robert Redford?

Why do actresses pose for *Playboy* in order to be taken more seriously by directors and producers?

Why are only young men

allowed to be angry?

Why is a woman allowed to behave as aggressively as a man only if she's suffering from PMS?

Is it because most women need drugs to cope with the pain of childbirth that men think of them as the weaker sex?

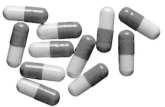

When men claim wearing a condom is a hardship, are they comparing it to giving birth or having an abortion?

Why are there vaginal deodorants

but no penis ones?

Have the men who claim that a woman's vagina smells unpleasant ever sniffed their own penises?

How come people describe tall buildings as "phallic" and then wonder why men think so highly of their penises?

Why do we say men "mentally" undress women, when the brain is not the organ engaged in the process?

Why doesn't vagina envy exist?

If women suffer from penis envy, why do men have more sex changes?

Why is women's underwear
marketed to men?

If fashion makes a statement,
why doesn't it ever say: "Leave
me alone, you dirty old man"?

If you can rape a woman for dressing like a whore, why can't you shoot a man for dressing like a thug?

If women get raped because they ask for it, why don't they ever get the equal pay, equal opportunities, and other things they ask for?

Why do men identify with Michael Douglas in *Fatal Attraction* when most stalking is done by men?

If hell hath no fury like a woman scorned, how come more men go to jail for murdering their ex-lovers?

Is it because men enjoy
the chase so much that
so many women have to
file restraining orders
against them?

If women are so much more "easy" these days, why are date-rape drugs so popular?

Is it because Rohypnol, the date-rape drug, costs less than five dollars a pop that men think women who have sex on the first date are "cheap"?

Why is it less of a crime to rape
a woman if the rapist takes her
out to dinner first?

Why are women warned to stay in at night for their own safety when home is the place they're most likely to be assaulted?

If all the good men are married,
who is committing the violence
that occurs in two-thirds of
all marriages?

If women are so eager for marriage, why do men have to get down on their knees to propose?

Why are romance novels dismissed as unrealistic when the romance and the story end once the heroine gets married?

Has it occurred to anyone that college-educated women over the age of thirty-five may be unmarried because they're smart?

If nice guys never get the girl, does that mean all women are married to bastards?

Why is there a "man shortage" when there are three billion of them?

Why, when surveys indicate single women are happier than married women, does the media portray the opposite?

Is her wedding the happiest day of a woman's life because she'll be miserable from then on?

If marriage is a trap for men,
why do women initiate the
majority of divorces?

Is the reason we hear of only women being stoned for adultery because there aren't enough rocks in the world for adulterous males?

Is the reason that only men practice polygamy that no wife would want more than one husband?

Is the reason a bridegroom isn't "given away" because nobody actually wants him?

Where are all the child *grooms*

and mail-order husbands?

Why is there a smart woman behind every successful man and a vacant space beside every successful woman?

Why are "trophy wives" rewards
for success and achievement
when "boy toys" are objects of
ridicule?

Why is a man only interested in a woman until she is interested in him?

Why do so many men start trying to make a relationship work after their partners have left them?

Why is it that if a man actively pursues a woman he's romantic, but if a woman actively pursues a man she's desperate?

Why is it that if a woman sleeps with lots of men she's a slut, but if she refuses to sleep with any of them she's a bitch?

Is it because 70 percent of the world's people living in poverty are female that men accuse women of being "needy"?

Is it because women only earn one-tenth of the world's wages that men accuse them of being after their money?

Is the reason most women don't like to admit they are feminists because it reduces their chances of getting a date with a chauvinist?

If people think feminists are man-hating lesbians, why don't they assume misogynists are gay?

Why do women need Ph.D.'s to be taken seriously as feminists when men don't need any qualifications to be successful chauvinists?

Why, if gender equality now
exists, is one gender still more
equal than the other?

Why would you have been less
likely to pick up this book had it been
titled *I Am a Feminist, And . . .* instead
of *I'm Not a Feminist, But . . . ?*